Chinese Language Proficiency Scales For Speakers of Other Languages

国际汉语能力标准

国家汉语国际推广领导小组办公室
The Office of Chinese Language Council International

Explanatory Introduction

1. Aims

Chinese Language Proficiency Scales for Speakers of Other Languages, drawn up to meet the needs of Chinese language teaching and learning worldwide, is a guideline document for teaching Chinese to speakers of other languages.

Designed for learners of Chinese as a foreign language, the Scales provide a five-band all-round description of their ability to use their knowledge and skills of the Chinese language for communication. It is an important basis on which the language proficiency of learners of Chinese can be measured.

The Scales can serve as a reference standard for drawing up a syllabus of teaching Chinese for speakers of other languages, for compiling Chinese textbooks, and for assessing the language proficiency of learners of Chinese.

2. Principle

The Scales have been established on the principle of drawing on the strengths of other language proficiency scales already developed internationally, taking theories of communicative competence as their foundation, focusing on the learner's actual use of the language and reflecting the characteristics of the Chinese language.

Language use usually takes the form of various activities or tasks. Linguistic activity can be divided into the receptive type (listening and reading), productive type (speaking and writing), interactive type (conversation and correspondence) and medium type (interpreting and translation). The Scales take the perspectives of the mode of communication and the process of communication to describe the learner's language proficiency in terms of "being able to do certain things". This truly reflects the actual use of the language and at the same time incorporates an important characteristic of the Chinese language, namely, that there is a marked difference between spoken and written Chinese.

3. Framework and content

The basic framework of the Scales comprises three levels (see figure below), each of which in turn consists of five bands.

Level one is an overview of the proficiency of Chinese as a foreign or second language. At this level a comprehensive description is provided of the language proficiency of a learner of Chinese in terms of listening, speaking, reading and writing.

Level two describes the Chinese language proficiency in terms of the spoken and written modes of communication, reflecting both the actual use of the language and the characteristics of learning Chinese.

Level three focuses on the process of comprehension and expression in linguistic communication, describing the learners' ability to comprehend spoken Chinese and express themselves orally and their ability to comprehend written Chinese and express themselves in writing.

Scales of Proficiency for Chinese as a Foreign or Second Language

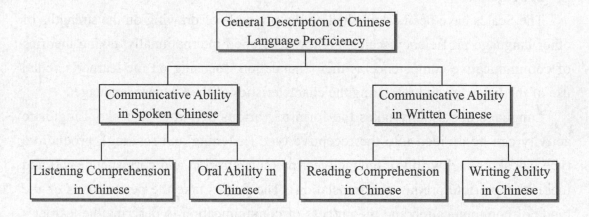

Description at Level three consists of description of language proficiency and exemplification of tasks. The description of language proficiency takes "being able to do certain things" as the starting point and describes the linguistic abilities involved in a communicative event, including:

(1) Listening comprehension, which comprises comprehending the interactive discourses in a social event/activity, comprehending instructive and explanatory discourses, and comprehending various informative discourses;

(2) Speaking, which comprises expressing oneself orally in a social interaction/ interactive situation, making oral statements, giving oral instructions, and explaining things and making requests orally;

(3) Reading comprehension, which comprises comprehending the correspondence in a social interaction, comprehending instructive and explanatory texts, and comprehending various kinds of informative texts;

(4) Writing, which comprises writing or replying to letters in a social interaction, recording, processing and conveying information in written form.

"Exemplification of tasks" cites the tasks of using Chinese that correspond to each band of language proficiency so as to facilitate the readers' understanding of the band of language proficiency that is described.

4. Developing the Scales

Since August 2006 the Office of Chinese Language Council International has commissioned language education experts and language testing experts from over 80 universities at home and abroad to take part in the research on drawing up the Scales and has solicited advice and opinion from a wide range of Chinese and overseas experts, scholars and teachers. Over 500 people have participated in this project. The research team have collected nearly 7,000 language use tasks at home and abroad; on the basis of features such as task difficulty and complexity, they have extracted the components that constitute language ability by means of qualitative and quantitative methods; they have established a bank of Chinese language proficiency descriptors and determined the bands of the Scales. The Scales have drawn on the results of research on international language proficiency scales such as Common European Framework of Reference for Languages: learning, teaching, assessment (CEFR) and Canadian Language Benchmarks (CLB).

It must be pointed out that the Scales provide a description of the ability of learners of Chinese as a foreign or second language to use the language, not a description of the language itself. As a common framework of reference for Chinese language teaching, learning, testing and assessment, the Scales do not provide the various knowledge and strategies that reflect the ability to use Chinese, such as vocabulary, grammar, etc. We are intensifying our efforts to establish the scales in this respect for use by learners, teachers and testers of Chinese.

We are deeply grateful to Professor Han Baocheng from the National Research Center for Foreign Language Education, Beijing Foreign Studies University, and to Professor Zhao Jinming from Beijing Language and Culture University, who, as leaders of the research team of this project, have made important contributions to the research on the Scales. We owe a special debt of gratitude to Professor Xu Jialu, Vice Chairman of the Standing Committee of the National People's Congress, who took time out of his extremely tight schedule to review the draft Scales and made many valuable comments. We are indebted to all the experts, scholars and teachers at home and abroad who have participated in this project and played a constructive role.

The establishment of the Scales is the first such attempt in the history of teaching Chinese as a foreign or second language. Due to time constraints and the lack of previous experience, there are bound to be shortcomings in the current version of the Scales, which can only be perfected in the process of its implementation. We would welcome the candid opinions and criticisms of our readers.

The Office of Chinese Language Council International
November 2007

Chinese Language Proficiency Scales for Speakers of Other Languages

Contents

I. General Description of Chinese Language Proficiency

Band	Description of Proficiency
1	Able approximately to comprehend simple, basic and very limited language material that is closely related to personal or everyday life. Able to introduce oneself or make oneself understood by others in very limited simple vocabulary with the help of body language or other means.
2	Able basically to comprehend simple and familiar language material that is closely related to personal or everyday life. Able to exchange ideas with others on common topics in relatively simple terms, such as describing the basic personal profile of oneself or others, sometimes having to resort to body language or other means.
3	Able to comprehend basic language material that is related to everyday life or work that would be encountered in a general communicative situation. Able to get one's ideas across or communicate with others on familiar topics, and able to give a simple description of the basic conditions that are related to the topics.
4	Able to comprehend language material with a clearly expressed familiar content which is encountered on a general social occasion or in a work or study situation, able to understand the important points and grasp the details. Able to communicate with others on familiar topics, expressing oneself clearly with a certain degree of coherence and using basic communicative strategies, and able to describe one's past experience, expressing one's opinions, giving simple reasons or explanations.
5	Able to comprehend general language material encountered on a variety of occasions in a variety of fields (including one's own field of speciality), able to grasp the important points and synthesize and analyse them. Able to take part fairly competently in communications and discussions on a wide variety of topics, including general topics in specialised fields, using a wide variety of communicative strategies to express one's opinion and attitude, and able to explain various opinions in a coherent and fairly appropriate manner.

II. Communicative Ability in Spoken Chinese

Band	Description of Proficiency
1	Able approximately to understand familiar, clearly articulated, simple and very brief oral discourse that is closely related to personal or everyday life, with the speaker often having to resort to body language and other means. Able to convey basic personal information in the simplest vocabulary, with one's mother tongue mingling in the discourse or with the help of body language in putting across one's meaning.
2	Able basically to understand simple, familiar and brief discourse that is closely related to personal or everyday life, understanding relevant information. Able to describe the basic information about oneself or others in very simple vocabulary, and able to exchange ideas with others on very familiar topics in a very simple manner.
3	Able to understand conversation or brief speech in everyday life or on general occasions, understanding the general idea and grasping the basic points. Able to get one's ideas across or communicate with others on relevant familiar topics or give a simple description in simple language.
4	Able to understand conversation or speech on familiar topics on a general occasion, grasping the main points and key information. Able to communicate with others on those topics by employing basic communicative strategies, expressing oneself quite clearly and with a certain degree of coherence.
5	Able to understand formal or informal conversation or speech on a wide variety of occasions including discussions about one's work or study, able to comprehend the main points, grasp the basic details, and find out the speaker's aims and intentions. Able to make oneself understood and communicate effectively with others on concrete or abstract topics and able to give a description or argumentation on a topic that one is interested in, expressing oneself clearly and coherently with appropriate details.

III. Communicative Ability in Written Chinese

Band	Description of Proficiency
1	Able to recognize a few characters or words in simple and very brief text messages that are closely related to personal or everyday life. Able to copy simple characters or words, fill in information that is closely related to personal life or provide very brief written answers to relevant questions in very simple basic vocabulary.
2	Able to recognize the main information in brief text messages that are commonly seen in personal or everyday life. Able to fill in information that is closely related to one's personal life or provide brief written answers to relevant questions in simple vocabulary.
3	Able to read short written material that is commonly seen in everyday life, work or study, understanding its main idea and recognizing specific information. Able to fill in information that is closely related to one's personal life or work, answer relevant questions or describe relevant conditions; able to carry out simple written communication on familiar topics in basic vocabulary or sentences on general occasions.
4	Able to read simple, easy and authentic written material on general occasions, obtaining the main points and key information. Able to make simple notes of what one reads or listens; able to give a brief description or explanation on familiar topics, including one's own past experience, in basically well-formed sentences, the language being basically clear and with a certain degree of coherence.
5	Able to read authentic ordinary written material of some length in work, daily life and study situations, understanding the main idea, grasping important facts and details, and displaying a knowledge of the structure of the text. On the basis of understanding written or spoken material, to be able to communicate with others in writing on some concrete topics or common abstract topics as is required, and to express one's personal opinion and point of view meaningfully in well-formed sentences in a coherent text.

IV. Listening Comprehension in Chinese

Band 1

Description of Proficiency	Exemplification of Tasks
• Able to understand simple words and phrases that are closely related to one's personal everyday life. • Able to understand basic numerals and the most common key words and phrases in a familiar environment. • Able to understand greetings or regards/well wishes from others. • Able to basically understand basic instructive remarks or requirements. • Able to understand simple remarks requesting repetition and clarification. • Often needing the interlocutor to resort to repetition, explanation or gesticulation.	• Listen to basic personal information. • Listen to the quantity and price of commodities. • Listen to simple instructions. • Listen to expressions of apology.

4

Band 2

Description of Proficiency	Exemplification of Tasks
• Able to understand clearly articulated simple words and phrases common in everyday life. • Able to understand simple discourse that is related to personal experiences. • Able to understand questions or simple instructions that are closely related to personal life. • Able to obtain from conversations concrete information involving numerals, time and places. • Often needing the interlocutor to resort to gesticulation or the aid of written material.	• Listen to the time and venue of an event. • Listen to someone introducing a new friend. • Listen to simple description of a commodity.

5

Listening Comprehension in Chinese

Band 3

Description of Proficiency	Exemplification of Tasks
• Able to understand brief conversation or exchange that is closely related to personal or everyday life. • Able to understand brief and direct questions that are related to personal experiences or concern common knowledge. • Able to understand questions or simple instructions that are closely related to personal life. • Able to obtain concrete information from casual conversation, introduction of a general nature or telephone conversation. • Able to understand simple stories, advertisements or the main idea of a newscast when the background to the news is familiar. • Occasionally needing the interlocutor to repeat or explain.	• Listen to someone describing his hobby. • Listen to description of community activities. • Listen to a brief description of a job or task. • Listen to description or a travel itinerary.

6

Listening Comprehension in Chinese

Band 4

Description of Proficiency	Exemplification of Tasks
• Able to understand standard and clearly articulated conversation or exchange in a general social situation, grasping the main idea and key information, and understanding the speaker's important points or intention. • Able to understand the main content of a discourse that is related to personal experiences and familiar topics. • Able to understand instructions, explanations or requests that are closely related to common topics. • Able to understand the main idea of a descriptive or declarative discourse. • Able to understand the main content of a newscast or a simple broadcast. • Occasionally needing the interlocutor to repeat.	• Listen to description of a school. • Listen to description of a product. • Listen to description of a house and its facilities. • Listen to brief newscast.

Listening Comprehension in Chinese

Band 5

Description of Proficiency	Exemplification of Tasks
• Able to understand clearly articulated speech or discourse uttered at a normal speed in a wide variety of social, everyday work or study environments, understanding the important points and grasping the details. • Able to understand a speech or discourse on a familiar topic but with a more abstract or complicated content, understanding its main idea and grasping the speaker's aim, attitude, etc. • Able to understand a clearly expressed description or explanation concerning a technical task. • Able to realize the implied meaning of someone's talk or speech.	• Listen to someone describing how something happened. • Listen to radio or television interviews. • Listen to a doctor describing a diagnosis. • Listen to someone's biographical account.

8

Listening Comprehension in Chinese

V. Oral Ability in Chinese

Band 1

Description of Proficiency	Exemplification of Tasks
• Able to greet others or respond to greetings from others. • Able to express the simplest information that has a direct bearing on oneself. • Able to express basic needs or give instructions by using a few words. • Able to make the most basic requests or seek help. • Often pausing and resorting to body language.	• Make utterances about basic personal information. • Ask about time and date. • Ask about a train schedule. • Ask about the interlocutor's address and telephone number.

9

Band 2

Description of Proficiency	Exemplification of Tasks
• Able to make oneself understood by others by limited means and to express one's basic needs. • Able to ask simple questions or give simple answers concerning very familiar topics in personal or everyday life. • Able to give simple instructions or make simple requests. • Able to provide basic information about oneself. • Sometimes pausing and resorting to body language.	• Ask about other people's hobbies. • Tell one's location. • Describe the features of a lost article. • Ask about travel arrangements.

10

Oral Ability in Chinese

Band 3

Description of Proficiency	Exemplification of Tasks
• Able to participate in brief or routine conversation and to discuss personal needs. • Able to make oneself understood by others, express one's needs or talk about one's past experiences. • Able to give a simple account of common activities in personal or everyday life. • Able to give simple instructions concerning matters in everyday life. • Able to give a simple description of a situation or condition or a simple account of an event. • Sometimes having to resort to gesticulation or the aid of relevant material.	• Describe one's colleagues or friends. • Describe one's holiday. • Answer a telephone or leave a message. • Ask about the functions of a commodity.

11

Oral Ability in Chinese

Band 4

Description of Proficiency	Exemplification of Tasks
• Able to communicate with others more confidently on general social occasions and to converse on common topics. • Able to participate in group discussions, make suggestions or proposals, give reasons, express one's opinions or point of view. • Able to make instructions concern-ing arrangements of everyday activities. • Able to describe briefly or report how something happened or the condition of something.	• Talk about one's work. • Describe one's eating habits. • Describe a special past experience one has had. • Compare the similarities and differences between two work units.

Oral Ability in Chinese

Band 5

Description of Proficiency	Exemplification of Tasks
• Able to converse and communicate with others effectively in a wide variety of social and work situations. • Able to make a presentation or participate in discussions on a general topic at a concrete or abstract level, able to state reasons and express one's opinion and attitude. • Able to describe, explain or instruct on a familiar operational process of a technical or non-technical nature.	• Describe the characteristics of a certain profession or trade. • Talk about a film that one likes. • Tell an anecdote about celebrity. • Present one's research topic.

Oral Ability in Chinese

VI. Reading Comprehension in Chinese

Band 1

Description of Proficiency	Exemplification of Tasks
• Able to read greetings and expressions of gratitude on general social occasions. • Able to understand the most basic numerals, characters, words or phrases that frequently occur in everyday life. • Able to understand approximately the most common instructions or signs that have obvious meanings and are clearly expressed.	• Recognize the personal names and place names in a picture or picture album. • Recognize commodity names. • Recognize the expressions of quantities of articles in a text. • Recognize names of tourist places.

Band 2

Description of Proficiency	Exemplification of Tasks
• Able to roughly understand brief texts such as those that express greetings, gratitude or an invitation, which are commonly encountered on social occasions. • Able to read familiar signs in everyday life and descriptive written materials that contain familiar characters and words and that arc often accompanied by figures, tables and charts. • Able to roughly understand general messages, notices or simple tables. • Able to detect a specific information from a brief text clearly written with a fixed format.	• Read a card of congratulations from a friend. • Read airport and train station schedules. • Read a course schedule/timetable. • Read a Lost & Found notice.

15

Reading Comprehension in Chinese

Band 3

Description of Proficiency	Exemplification of Tasks
• Able to read messages, records, e-mails, text messages or brief letters on general social occasions. • Able to read simple short descriptive or explanatory texts in everyday life. • Able to read simple narrative or descriptive texts that are closely related to everyday life or have a predictable content, grasping the main and concrete information. • Able to find specific information that one needs from longer texts with a familiar content.	• Read private correspondence. • Read job advertisements. • Read brief conference notices. • Read simple short stories.

16

Reading Comprehension in Chinese

Band 4

Description of Proficiency	Exemplification of Tasks
• Able to read written texts for general social purposes such like ordinary letters, e-mails, notices, grasping the key information contained. • Able to read ordinary descriptive or explanatory texts in everyday life. • Ablc to read descriptive or narrative short texts on familiar and real-life topics written in simple language, able to grasp the central issue, theme and some important details, and to understand the intention of the author. • Able to read longer texts that contain mainly factual information and locate the specific information that one needs.	• Read posters on a campus. • Read brief introductions to new books. • Read the tourist guidebook of a certain place. • Browse through a guidebook about a certain country.

17

Reading Comprehension in Chinese

Band 5

Description of Proficiency	Exemplification of Tasks
• Able to read and understand letters or other types of practical writing found in work, daily life and study situations, including the working documents within certain operational domains, and to understand accurately their content. • Able to read general newspaper or magazine articles, contemporary novels and academic or business texts, understanding the central issue, theme, key information or important details of the texts. • Able to read and understand texts of some lengths or more complicated descriptive or explanatory texts, to be able to grasp their gist and find specific information that one needs. • Able to read and understand abstract, conceptual or technical texts, able to grasp the facts and important points, read between the lines and understand the viewpoints or intention of the author.	• Browse through leisure magazines. • Read popular science articles. • Read biographies and autobiographies. • Read business texts.

18

Reading Comprehension in Chinese

VII. Writing Ability in Chinese

Band 1

Description of Proficiency	Exemplification of Tasks
• Able to write simple phrases for social purposes, such as greetings on greeting cards or cards of congratulations, addresses on envelopes and so on with basically correct characters. • Able to copy and record time, personal names, numerals, and prices. • Able to fill in a form with the most relevant personal information in simple characters and words.	• Fill in personal names. • Copy addresses. • Fill in time. • Fill in occupations.

Band 2

Description of Proficiency	Exemplification of Tasks
• Able to express gratitude, apology, congratulations, farewell, etc. in simple words or sentences. • Able to record, fill in, or copy basic information that is closely related to oneself, one's family or one's life. • Able to give brief answers to simple questions that are closely related to one's personal life.	• Copy commodity names and prices. • Write a greeting card or card of congratulations. • Make a shopping list. • Write a message.

Writing Ability in Chinese

Band 3

Description of Proficiency	Exemplification of Tasks
• Able to write short messages on familiar topics for general social purposes. • Able to record, copy or fill in factual or descriptive messages. • Able to give a simple description, narrating a very familiar event, story or a plan or something that is closely related to oneself or one's family.	• Write a greeting card or card of congratulations. • Write a letter of thanks. • Fill in a simple application form. • Write a description of one's personal details.

Writing Ability in Chinese

Band 4

Description of Proficiency	Exemplification of Tasks
• Able to write texts of some lengths on the common topics in everyday life, study or social activities in accordance with certain format, convey or express information in an appropriate manner. • Able to note down important information that one hears or reads, able to take notes of a brief oral report or reference material. • Able to describe, explain or narrate one's personal experiences or on familiar topics in basically well-formed sentences and to express things clearly.	• Take minutes of a small meeting. • Write an abstract or summary of a text. • Narrate a story. • Describe a picture.

Writing Ability in Chinese

国际汉语能力标准

Chinese Language Proficiency Scales
For Speakers of Other Languages

国家汉语国际推广领导小组办公室
The Office of Chinese Language Council International

编 委 会

主任：许　琳

委员（以姓氏笔画为序）：

马箭飞、白乐桑（法国）、刘润清、陈国华、赵国成、
赵金铭、韩宝成

研 制 组

组长：韩宝成、赵金铭、许　琳、赵国成、马箭飞

主要参与人员（以姓氏笔画为序）：

马燕华	（北京师范大学）
毛　悦	（北京语言大学）
艾力山	（保加利亚索菲亚大学）
白瑞凡	（意大利威尼斯大学）
冯子平	（加拿大汤姆逊大学）
冯　睿	（加拿大阿尔伯塔大学）
刘长征	（北京语言大学）
刘　壮	（首都师范大学）
李充阳	（韩国韩中文化协力研究院）
李　泉	（中国人民大学）
李祖清	（缅甸曼德勒福庆学校）
李端端	（加拿大不列颠哥伦比亚大学）
李赛红	（丹麦哥本哈根商业大学）
杨承青	（国家汉办）
吴中伟	（复旦大学）
吴　华	（加拿大休伦大学学院）
邱　宁	（国家汉办）
佟涤非	（泰国东方文化书院）
佘嘉元	（南京师范大学）

迟兰英　　　　　　（北京语言大学）

张希春　　　　　　（北京外国语大学）

张和生　　　　　　（北京师范大学）

张晋军　　　　　　（国家汉办）

陈青海　　　　　　（美国密西根大学）

陈　琪　　　　　　（新加坡中国汉语水平考试中心〈科思达〉）

林秀琴　　　　　　（首都师范大学）

欧阳荣华　　　　　（美国肯尼索州立大学）

罗陈霞　　　　　　（对外经济贸易大学）

罗青松　　　　　　（中国人民大学）

罗　相　　　　　　（澳大利亚斯特斯·费尔德学院）

周小兵　　　　　　（中山大学）

周高宇　　　　　　（国家汉办）

赵　杨　　　　　　（北京大学）

赵秀娟　　　　　　（北京语言大学）

胡荣安　　　　　　（日本青少年育成协会）

柯拉拉　　　　　　（意大利米兰大学）

柯佩琦　　　　　　（瑞士苏黎世大学）

饶　勤　　　　　　（首都师范大学）

姜丽萍　　　　　　（北京语言大学）

徐　弘　　　　　　（加拿大埃德蒙顿公立教育局）

常海潮　　　　　　（北京外国语大学）

鹿士义　　　　　　（北京大学）

谢小庆　　　　　　（北京语言大学）

谢　广　　　　　　（泰国南邦公立育华学校）

谢绵绵　　　　　　（加拿大埃德蒙顿公立教育局）

戴海琦　　　　　　（江西师范大学）

魏崇新　　　　　　（北京外国语大学）

说　明

一、目的

　　《国际汉语能力标准》（以下简称《标准》）是为适应各国汉语教学需求制订的，是指导国际汉语教学的纲领性文件。

　　《标准》面向汉语作为外语的学习者，对其运用汉语知识和技能进行交际的能力，从不同层面提供了五个级别的描述，是衡量汉语学习者语言能力的重要依据。

　　《标准》可作为制订国际汉语教学大纲、编写教材和测评汉语学习者语言能力的参照标准。

二、原则

　　制订《标准》的原则是：借鉴国际语言能力标准的研制成果，以交际语言能力理论为指导，注重语言的实际运用，同时体现汉语自身特点。

　　语言运用通常是以各种活动或任务的方式出现的。语言活动的类型可分为接收型（听、读）、产出型（说、写）、互动型（对话和书信往来等）和中介型（口译、笔译）。《标准》从不同交际方式和交际过程入手，以"能做某事"作为语言能力描述的出发点，真实反映语言的实际运用，同时体现口语和书面语之间存在较大区别这一汉语的特点。

三、框架与内容

　　《标准》的基本框架由三个层面（见下图）组成，每个层面分五个级别。

　　第一层面是国际汉语能力总体描述。该层面对把汉语作为外语的学习者在听、说、读、写活动中所表现的语言能力进行综合描述。

　　第二层面分别从口头和书面两种交际方式的角度对汉语能力进行描述，既体现了语言运用的实际状况，也反映了汉语学习的特点。

　　第三层面从语言交际理解与表达的过程入手，分别对汉语口头理解和表达能力、汉语书面理解和表达能力进行描述。

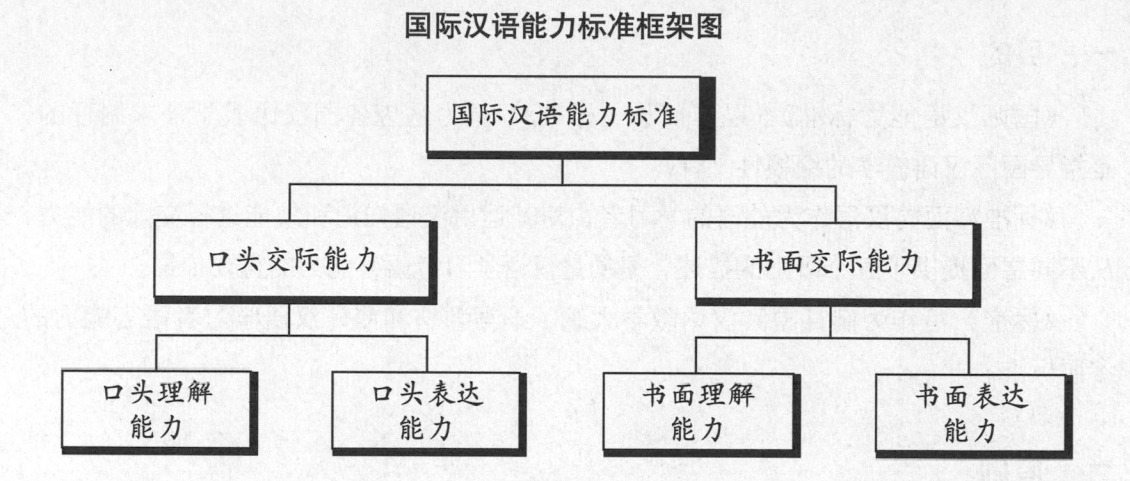

国际汉语能力标准框架图

第三层面的描述由语言能力描述和任务举例组成。"语言能力描述"以"能做某事"为出发点,对每一交际过程涉及的语言能力进行描述,包括:

1. 口头理解能力,涵盖对社交场合互动话语的理解,对指示性、说明性话语的理解,对各种信息类话语的理解;

2. 口头表达能力,涵盖社交场合的互动型口头表达,口头给出指示、说明或要求,陈述与表达信息;

3. 书面理解能力,涵盖对社交场合往来函件的理解,对指示性或说明性文本的理解,对各种信息类文本的理解;

4. 书面表达能力,涵盖社交场合往来函件的撰写,信息的记录、加工与书面传达。

"任务举例"列举与各语言能力级别相对应的汉语应用任务的实例,以便于读者对所描述语言能力级别的理解。

四、研制过程

自 2006 年 8 月起,国家汉语国际推广领导小组办公室(Hanban)先后组织海内外八十多所大学的语言教学专家及教育测量专家参与《标准》的研制工作,并广泛征求了国内外专家学者和教师的意见,参与者达五百多人。研制组在国内外先后收集了近七千条语言应用任务,根据任务的难度、复杂度等特征并采用定性和定量的方法提取出构成语言能力的要素,建立起汉语能力描述库并确定了《标准》的级别。《标准》借鉴了 CEFR(Common European Framework of Reference for Languages: learning,

teaching, assessment)、CLB（Canadian Language Benchmarks）等国际语言能力标准的研制成果。

　　需要指出的是,《标准》是对汉语作为外语或第二语言学习者使用汉语能力的描述,不是对汉语本身的描述。作为汉语教学、学习及评测的共同参考框架,《标准》尚未提供反映汉语使用能力的各种知识和策略,如词汇、语法等。我们正在抓紧制订这方面的标准,以便汉语学习者、教师、测试工作者等人士使用。

　　北京外国语大学中国外语教育研究中心韩宝成教授和北京语言大学赵金铭教授作为本项目研制组牵头人,为《标准》的研制做出了重要贡献,我们深表感谢。全国人民代表大会常务委员会副委员长许嘉璐教授在百忙之中对《标准》进行了审阅,提出了许多宝贵意见,对此我们特别感谢。我们还要感谢所有参与过本项研究并发挥了建设性作用的海内外专家、学者和教师。

　　《标准》的研制在汉语作为外语或第二语言教学的历史上尚属首次。由于时间短,缺乏经验,目前的《标准》必然存在一些不足之处,有待在实施过程中臻于完善,欢迎广大读者提出宝贵意见。

国家汉语国际推广领导小组办公室

2007 年 11 月

国际汉语能力标准

目　录

一、汉语能力总体描述

等级划分	能力描述
一级	能大体理解与个人或日常生活密切相关的简单、基础而又十分有限的语言材料。借助肢体语言或其他手段的帮助，能用非常有限的简单语汇介绍自己或与他人沟通。
二级	能基本理解与个人或日常生活密切相关的熟悉而简单的语言材料。能就常见话题以较简单的方式与他人沟通，介绍自己或他人的基本情况，有时需借助肢体语言或其他手段的帮助。
三级	能理解与日常生活和工作相关的以及在一般交际场合中遇到的基本的语言材料。能就熟悉的话题与他人进行沟通和交流，能对与这些话题相关的基本情况作简单描述。
四级	能理解在一般社交场合或在工作、学习等场合遇到的表达清晰、内容熟悉的语言材料，抓住重点，把握细节。能就熟悉的话题与他人进行交流，表述清楚且有一定连贯性，会使用基本的交际策略。能描述自己的经历，表达自己的看法，给出简单的理由或解释。
五级	能理解多种场合、多种领域（包括个人专业领域）的普通语言材料，能够把握重点，进行概括和分析。能使用多种交际策略较自如地参与多种话题，包括专业领域内一般性话题的交流和讨论，表明自己的观点和态度，并能对各种意见进行阐释，表达连贯，基本得体。

1

二、汉语口头交际能力

等级划分	能力描述
一级	能大体听懂与个人或日常生活密切相关的熟悉、清晰、简单并十分简短的话语，说话者常需借助肢体语言或其他手段的帮助。能用最简单的语汇传达关于个人的基本信息，话语中可能夹杂母语，或借助肢体语言表达自己的意思。
二级	能基本听懂与个人或日常生活密切相关的熟悉而简短的话语，抓住相关信息。能用非常简单的语汇介绍自己或他人的基本情况。能十分简单地就日常生活中非常熟悉的话题与他人沟通。
三级	能听懂日常生活或一般场合下的交谈或简短发言，明白其大意，把握基本情况。能就与此相关的熟悉话题用简单的话语与他人进行沟通和交流，或作简单描述。
四级	能听懂一般场合下关于熟悉话题的交谈或发言，抓住主要内容和关键信息。能使用基本的交际策略就这些话题与他人进行交流，表达基本清楚，且有一定的连贯性。
五级	能听懂多种场合下的正式或非正式的交谈或发言，包括与自己工作或学习相关的讨论，能抓住要点，把握基本情况，明白说话人的目的和意图。能在多种场合下与他人就具体或抽象的话题进行有效的沟通和交流，并能就自己感兴趣的话题进行描述或论证，表达清楚连贯，详略得当。

三、汉语书面交际能力

等级划分	能力描述
一级	能识别与个人或日常生活密切相关的简短信息类材料中的少数单字或短语。能抄写简单的字词，用非常简单的基本词汇填写与个人生活密切相关的信息或极简短地书面回答相关问题。
二级	能识别个人或日常生活中常见简短信息类材料中的主要信息。能用简单的语汇填写与个人生活密切相关的信息或简短地书面回答相关问题。
三级	能阅读日常生活、工作或学习中常见的简短书面材料，了解大意，识别具体信息。能填写与个人生活或工作密切相关的信息，回答相关问题或介绍相关情况。能用最基本的语汇或句子就一般场合下熟悉的话题进行简单的书面交流。
四级	能看懂一般场合下浅显、真实的书面语言材料，获取主要内容和关键信息。能对所读或所听的材料作简单记录。能就熟悉的话题，包括自己的经历，作简单描述或说明，语句基本通顺，表达基本清楚，且有一定连贯性。
五级	能理解工作、生活或学习等场合中有一定长度、普通、真实的书面语言材料，抓住大意，掌握重要事实和细节，了解文本的结构。在理解书面或口头材料的基础上，能根据要求，就一些具体话题或常见的抽象话题与他人进行书面交流，或发表个人的意见与看法，言之有物，语句通顺，语篇连贯。

3

四、汉语口头理解能力

一级

能力描述	任务举例
• 能听懂与个人日常生活密切相关的简单词语。 • 能听懂所熟悉的环境中基本的数字和最常用的关键词语。 • 能听懂他人的问候或招呼。 • 能明白基本的指示话语或要求。 • 能明白要求重复和澄清的简单话语。 • 常需会话对方重复、解释或借助手势等。	• 听基本个人信息。 • 听商品数量、价格。 • 听简单的指令。 • 听表示抱歉的话。

二级

能力描述	任务举例
• 能听懂日常生活中常见的简单、清晰的话语。 • 能听懂与个人经历相关的简单话语。 • 理解与个人生活密切相关的问题或简单的指示。 • 能获取交谈中涉及的数字、时间、地点等具体信息。 • 常需会话对方借助手势或书面材料。	• 听事件发生的时间和地点。 • 听他人简单介绍一位新朋友。 • 听常见商品的简单介绍。

汉语口头理解能力

三级

能力描述	任务举例
• 能听懂与个人或日常生活密切相关的简短会话或交谈。 • 能听懂与个人经历有关或一般常识相关的简短且直接的问题。 • 能听懂日常生活中常见的指示要求或话语。 • 能了解闲谈、一般性介绍或电话交谈中的具体信息。 • 能听懂简单的故事、广告或熟悉其背景情况的新闻广播中的主要内容。 • 偶尔需要会话对方解释或重复。	• 听别人介绍自己的爱好。 • 听社团活动介绍。 • 听工作任务简介。 • 听旅行计划介绍。

汉语口头理解能力

四级

能力描述	任务举例
<ul><li>能听懂一般社交场合标准、清晰的对话或交谈，抓住主要内容和关键信息，领悟说话人话语的重点或意图。</li><li>能听懂表述清楚的与个人经历和熟悉话题相关话语的主要内容。</li><li>能听懂与常见话题相关的指示、说明或要求。</li><li>能理解描述性或陈述性话语的大意。</li><li>能听懂新闻播报中的主要内容或其他简单的广播。</li><li>偶尔需要会话对方重复。</li></ul>	<ul><li>听学校情况介绍。</li><li>听产品介绍。</li><li>听房屋设施介绍。</li><li>听简短新闻广播。</li></ul>

7

汉语口头理解能力

五级

能力描述	任务举例
• 能在许多社交、日常工作或学习环境中听懂他人语速正常、话语清晰的讲话或发言，抓住重点并掌握细节。 • 能听懂话题熟悉但内容抽象或复杂的讲话或发言，抓住主要内容，掌握讲话者的目的、态度等。 • 能听懂清楚的有关技术性任务的说明或讲解。 • 能领悟他人谈话或发言中暗含的意思。	• 听某人讲述事情发生的经过。 • 听广播或电视访谈节目。 • 听医生介绍诊治情况。 • 听某人的生平介绍。

汉语口头理解能力

五、汉语口头表达能力

一级

能力描述	任务举例
• 能问候他人或对他人的问候作出回应。 • 能说出与个人直接相关的最简单信息。 • 能用几个词表达基本的需求或给出指示。 • 能表达最基本的请求或寻求帮助。 • 经常停顿且依赖肢体语言。	• 说出个人基本信息。 • 询问时间、日期。 • 询问列车时刻。 • 询问对方地址及电话。

二级

能力描述	任务举例
<ul><li>能以有限的方式与他人沟通，表达基本的需求。</li><li>能就个人或日常生活中非常熟悉的话题提出简单的问题或给出简单的回答。</li><li>能给出简单的指示或要求。</li><li>能说出个人的基本信息。</li><li>有停顿且依赖肢体语言。</li></ul>	<ul><li>询问他人的爱好。</li><li>说出自己身处的方位。</li><li>描述丢失物品的特点。</li><li>询问旅游安排。</li></ul>

汉语口头表达能力

三级

能力描述	任务举例
• 能参与简短或例行的对话，讨论个人需求。 • 能和他人沟通，说出自己的需求或经历。 • 能简单描述个人或日常生活中常见的活动。 • 能就日常生活中的一些事务给出简单的指示。 • 能简单描述某一状况，讲述简单的事件。 • 有时需借助手势或相关辅助材料。	• 介绍自己的同事或朋友。 • 介绍自己的假期生活。 • 接听电话或留言。 • 询问商品功能。

汉语口头表达能力

四级

能力描述	任务举例
• 能在一般社交场合较自信地与他人交流，就常见话题进行交谈。 • 能参加小组讨论，就某件事情提出建议、给出理由、表达自己的观点或意见。 • 能就简单的日常活动安排作出指示。 • 能简单描述或报告某件事情的经过或情况。	• 谈论自己的工作。 • 说明自己的饮食习惯。 • 描述自己的一次特殊经历。 • 比较两个单位的异同。

汉语口头表达能力

五级

能力描述	任务举例
● 能在多数社交和工作场合自信并有效地与他人交谈、交流。 ● 能就一般性话题在具体或抽象层面进行讲述或参与讨论，能陈述理由，表明观点和态度。 ● 能对熟悉的技术或非技术性工作流程作出说明、解释或指示。	● 介绍某种职业的特点。 ● 谈论自己喜欢的电影。 ● 讲述名人逸事。 ● 陈述自己的研究课题。

汉语口头表达能力

六、汉语书面理解能力

一级

能力描述	任务举例
• 能基本看懂一般社交场合问候语和感谢语。 • 能大体理解日常生活中经常出现的、最基本的数字、字词或话语。 • 能大体理解最常见的、意义明显且清楚的指示语或标识。	• 识别图片、画册中的人名、地名等。 • 识别商品名称。 • 识别文本中所表达的物品数量。 • 识别旅游地点的名称。

二级

能力描述	任务举例
• 能基本认读和理解常见社交场合表示问候、感谢或邀请类的简短文字材料。 • 能看懂日常生活中熟悉的标识以及含有熟悉字词的、简单的、常附有图表的说明性材料。 • 能大体看懂一般的便条、通知或简单的表格。 • 能在表述清楚、格式固定的简短材料中找到某一特定信息。	• 看朋友贺卡。 • 看机场、车站时刻表。 • 看课程表。 • 看寻物启事。

三级

能力描述	任务举例
• 能读懂一般社交场合的留言、记录、电子邮件、短信或简短信函。 • 能看懂日常生活中简短的介绍性或说明性材料。 • 能读懂与日常生活密切相关或内容可预测的简单的叙述性或描写性材料,抓住主要的和具体的信息。 • 能在内容熟悉的稍长文本中找到所需的特定信息。	• 读私人信件。 • 看招聘启事。 • 看简短的会议通知。 • 读简短的小故事。

汉语书面理解能力

四级

能力描述	任务举例
• 能读懂社交场合普通的信函、电子邮件、通知等文字材料，掌握其关键信息。 • 能看懂日常生活中普通的介绍性或说明性材料。 • 能看懂一般场合中语言浅显、话题熟悉而又真实的描述性或叙述性短文，能抓住中心议题、主旨和某些重要细节，领悟作者意图。 • 能阅读以事实性信息为主的较长文本，从中找到所需的特定信息。	• 看校内海报。 • 查阅新书简介。 • 看某地旅游指南。 • 浏览某国概况。

五级

能力描述	任务举例
• 能读懂工作、生活或学习等场合有一定长度的信函或其他类应用文，包括一定业务范围内的工作文件，准确理解其内容。 • 能阅读一般性报纸或杂志文章、当代小说及学术性或商业性材料，抓住所读材料的中心议题、主旨、关键信息或重要细节。 • 能看懂有一定长度的材料或相当复杂的介绍性或说明性材料，能掌握梗概，从中找到所需特定信息。 • 能读懂抽象的、概念性的或技术性的材料，能把握事实，掌握要点，领会字里行间的意思及作者的观点或意图。	• 翻阅生活杂志。 • 阅读科普文章。 • 阅读人物传记。 • 阅读商务文本。

汉语书面理解能力

七、汉语书面表达能力

一级

能力描述	任务举例
<ul><li>能书写社交场合中的简单用语，如贺卡上的问候语、信封上的地址等，书写基本正确。</li><li>能抄写、记录时间、姓名、数字或价钱。</li><li>能用简单的字词填写与个人信息最相关的表格。</li></ul>	<ul><li>填写姓名。</li><li>抄写地址。</li><li>填写时间。</li><li>填写职业。</li></ul>

二级

能力描述	任务举例
• 能用简单的语汇或句子表达感谢、道歉、祝贺、告别等。 • 能记录、填写或抄写与自己、家庭或生活密切相关的基本信息。 • 能简短回答与个人生活密切相关的简单问题。	• 抄写商品名称、价格。 • 填写贺卡。 • 写购物清单。 • 写留言条。

汉语书面表达能力

三级

能力描述	任务举例
• 能就一般社交场合下熟悉的话题书写简短的信息。 • 能记录、抄写或填写事实性或说明性信息。 • 能简单叙述与个人、家庭有关的或其他非常熟悉的事件、故事、计划等。	• 写贺卡。 • 写感谢信。 • 填写简单申请表格。 • 写个人情况介绍。

四级

能力描述	任务举例
• 能就日常生活、学习或社交中的常见话题按一定格式书写一定长度的文字，恰当地传递或表达信息。 • 能记下听到或读到的重要信息，能根据简短的口头报告或参考资料作简单笔记。 • 能对个人经历或熟悉的话题、材料进行描述、说明或叙述，语句基本通顺，表达基本清楚。	• 作小型会议记录。 • 写文本摘要或概要。 • 叙述一个故事。 • 描述一幅图片。

汉语书面表达能力

五级

能力描述	任务举例
<ul><li>能撰写一般场合或一定工作范围内的应用文或普通工作文件，格式正确，语言表达清楚、通顺。</li><li>能对听到或读到的材料进行总结，有条理地写出说明、摘要或简要报告。</li><li>能够撰写一般性文章，就具体或一般性抽象话题进行描述、阐释或说明，用词恰当，表达通顺。能正确反映客观情况，表达自己的观点。</li></ul>	<ul><li>写读书感想。</li><li>写说明文。</li><li>写详细工作报告。</li><li>描述一件事。</li></ul>

汉语书面表达能力

Band 5

Description of Proficiency	Exemplification of Tasks
• Able to write a practical piece of writing or an ordinary work report for general purposes or within a certain domain of work with the correct format and in clear and appropriate and fluent language. • Able to summarize what one has heard or read, write a description, abstract or brief report in an orderly manner. • Able to write articles of a general nature, give descriptions, expositions or explanations on general abstract topics, with appropriate wording and in well-formed sentences; able to correctly reflect the objective situation and express one's opinions.	• Write about one's feelings and thoughts after reading a book. • Write an exposition. • Write a detailed work report. • Describe an event.

23

Writing Ability in Chinese